DREAMWORKS

HOW TO TRAIN YOUR

DRAGON 2

COLORING & ACTIVITY BOOK

bendon

CODEBREAKER

Using the secret code below, fill in the blanks and reveal the hidden words.

C O N T R O L

T H E

A L P H A

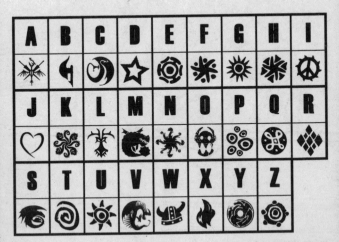

A	B	C	D	E	F	G	H	I
J	K	L	M	N	O	P	Q	R
S	T	U	V	W	X	Y	Z	

PICK A PIECE

Color the piece that completes the puzzle below.

A   **B**   **C**

ANSWER: Piece B

GRID
DRAW

Using the grid as a guide,
copy the picture in the grid below.

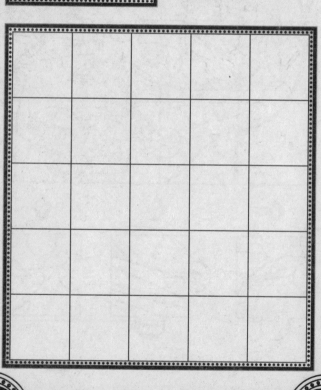

CLOSE-UPS

Match the characters by writing the correct number below each close-up.

1

2

3

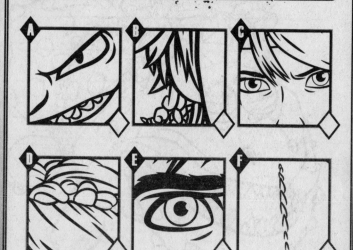

A

B

C

D

E

F

WORD COUNT

How many words can you make using the letters from...

THE CLASH OF FIRE AND ICE

Example: race

MAZE ESCAPE

Help Hiccup through the maze and back to Toothless.

START

FINISH

PICK A PIECE

Color the piece that completes the puzzle below.

WORD COUNT

How many words can you make using the letters from...

FASTEST DRAGON ALIVE

Example: fire

_____   _____

_____   _____

_____   _____

_____   _____

_____   _____

_____   _____

_____   _____

_____   _____

_____   _____

_____   _____

_____   _____

PICK A PIECE

Color the piece that completes the puzzle below.

A B C

WORD SEARCH

Find the words from the list in the puzzle below.

```
I E A N U Y D G V Q H
T U J S B A K D Y K I
A W V F T U X B T I C
Z Z A U Q R O W Y W C
Q S V W V F I W E W U
V P N M M I J D Y T P
Y Y K O H S Z Z H U N
L H R J T H D G S F O
V C K N V L D M X F O
I V H R W E O F G N H
M J H Y I G F U S U V
J E K H E S R Q T T C
```

═══ WORD LIST ═══

~~ASTRID~~ ~~FISHLEGS~~ ~~HICCUP~~ ~~SNOTLOUT~~ ~~TUFFNUT~~

RIDER MATCH

Draw a line between the rider and his or her dragon.

CODEBREAKER

Using the secret code below, fill in the blanks and reveal the hidden words.

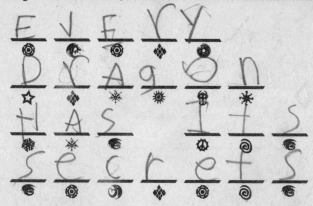

E V E R Y

D R A G O N

H A S I T S

S E C R E T S

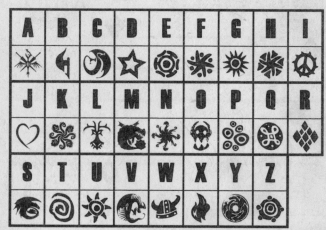

A	B	C	D	E	F	G	H	I

J	K	L	M	N	O	P	Q	R

S	T	U	V	W	X	Y	Z

WORD COUNT

How many words can you make using the letters from...

NOT YOUR AVERAGE DRAGON

Example: great

_____   _____

_____   _____

_____   _____

_____   _____

_____   _____

_____   _____

_____   _____

_____   _____

_____   _____

_____   _____

_____   _____

PICK A PIECE

Color the piece that completes the puzzle below.

GRID DRAW

Using the grid as a guide,
copy the picture in the grid below.

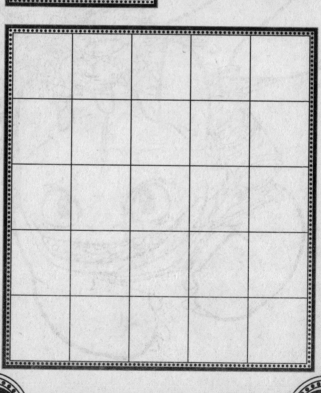

WORD SEARCH

Find the words from the list in the puzzle below.

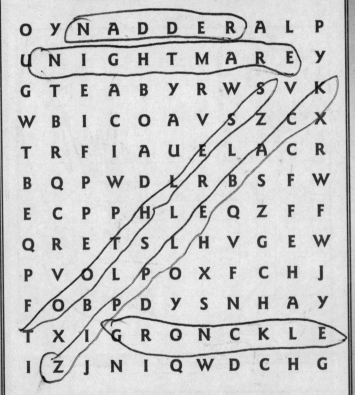

```
O  Y  N  A  D  D  E  R  A  L  P
U  N  I  G  H  T  M  A  R  E  Y
G  T  E  A  B  Y  R  W  S  V  K
W  B  I  C  O  A  V  S  Z  C  X
T  R  F  I  A  U  E  L  A  C  R
B  Q  P  W  D  L  R  B  S  F  W
E  C  P  P  H  L  E  Q  Z  F  F
Q  R  E  T  S  L  H  V  G  E  W
P  V  O  L  P  O  X  F  C  H  J
F  O  B  P  D  Y  S  N  H  A  Y
T  X  I  G  R  O  N  C  K  L  E
I  Z  J  N  I  Q  W  D  C  H  G
```

═══ WORD LIST ═══

~~GRONCKLE~~ ~~NADDER~~ ~~NIGHTMARE~~ ~~TOOTHLESS~~ ZIPPLEBACK

MAZE ESCAPE

Help Toothless through the maze and back to Hiccup.

START

FINISH

CLOSE-UPS

Match the characters by writing the correct number below each close-up.

1

2

3

How To Train Your Dragon 2 © 2014 DreamWorks Animation L.L.C.

SQUARES

With a friend, take turns connecting a line from one dot to another.
Whoever makes the line that completes a square puts their initial inside
the square. The person with the most squares at the end of the game wins.

WORD COUNT

How many words can you make using the letters from...

CONTROL THE ALPHA

Example: trap

WORD SEARCH

Find the words from the list in the puzzle below.

```
M A S X C X G W W C R
A T E B U F K R E A R
T A H T F S E L D L S
U E O Y E N I N G S S
F A W Y N A O T M P T
P X H I S G M S K E U
R J W E A W S D U I N
N R O R R R T V S K T
I Y D G E Z W G Y K S
S U P C Y V H P W Q A
N E A N Z L O O D Z E
G R D S Y P C R T O U
```

═══◆═══ **WORD LIST** ═══◆═══

~~DRAGON~~   RACERS   STUNTS   TEAM   WINNER

MAZE ESCAPE

Help Fishlegs through the maze and back to Meatlug.

START

FINISH

CODEBREAKER

Using the secret code below, fill in the blanks and reveal the hidden words.

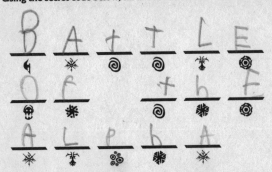

B A T T L E
O F   T H E
A L P H A

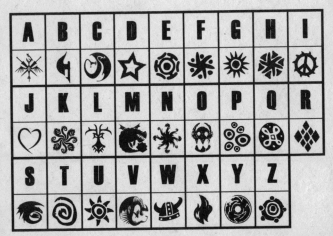

A	B	C	D	E	F	G	H	I
J	K	L	M	N	O	P	Q	R
S	T	U	V	W	X	Y	Z	

RIDER MATCH

Draw a line between the rider and his or her dragon.

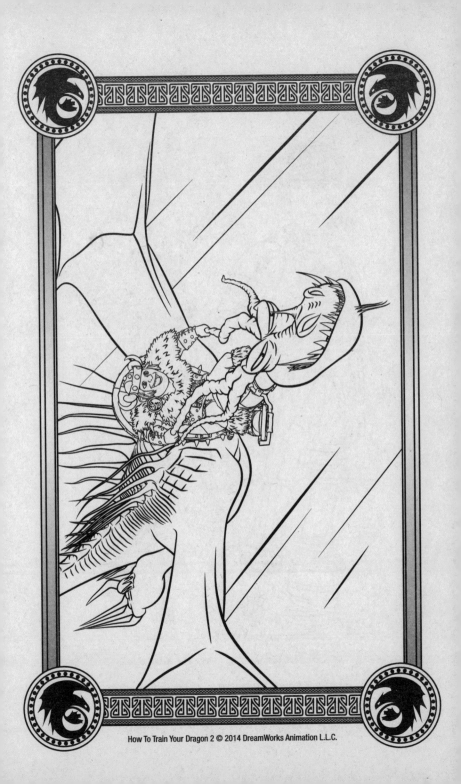

GRID DRAW

Using the grid as a guide,
copy the picture in the grid below.

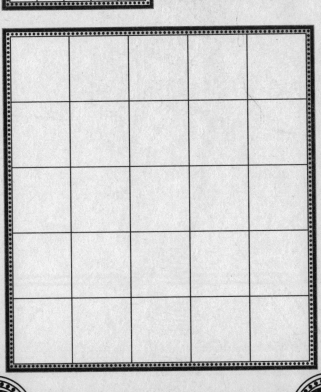

SQUARES

With a friend, take turns connecting a line from one dot to another.
Whoever makes the line that completes a square puts their initial inside
the square. The person with the most squares at the end of the game wins.

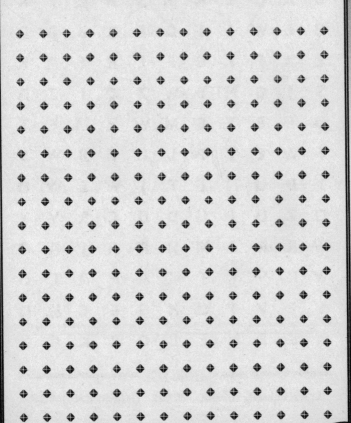

WORD SEARCH

Find the words from the list in the puzzle below.

```
G  X  O  E  A  M  S  H  Q  F  R
B  E  W  I  L  D  E  R  B  A  D
Z  X  F  F  G  F  E  H  T  A  K
S  J  G  N  B  W  Z  O  I  Z  A
D  L  E  T  C  M  W  P  M  F  T
F  W  E  T  P  L  U  F  B  W  S
Y  D  U  N  L  T  J  W  E  W  O
Q  Z  U  I  U  D  D  C  R  V  Y
W  R  A  M  H  R  A  J  A  Q
W  K  V  F  T  K  A  R  A  L  O
S  E  V  Y  U  H  G  E  C  K  Q
X  K  E  N  E  B  O  R  K  A  Y
```

◆━━ WORD LIST ━━◆

BEWILDERBAD DRAGO SKRILL TIMBERJACK VALKA

TIC-TAC-TOE

Use these grids to challenge your friends.

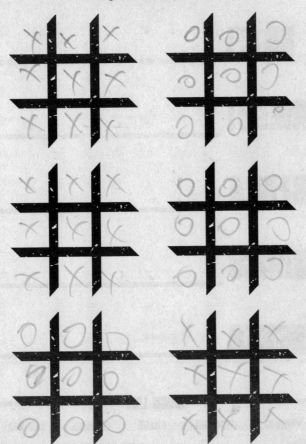

UNSCRAMBLE

Rearrange the scrambled letters to reveal the hidden words.

BRTEI _Tribe_

NIKGVI _Viking_

REDBA _bread_

RHNSO _Horns_

HGUTO _tough_

WORD LIST

VIKING   TOUGH   TRIBE   HORNS   BEARD

MAZE ESCAPE

Make your way to the center of the maze.

START

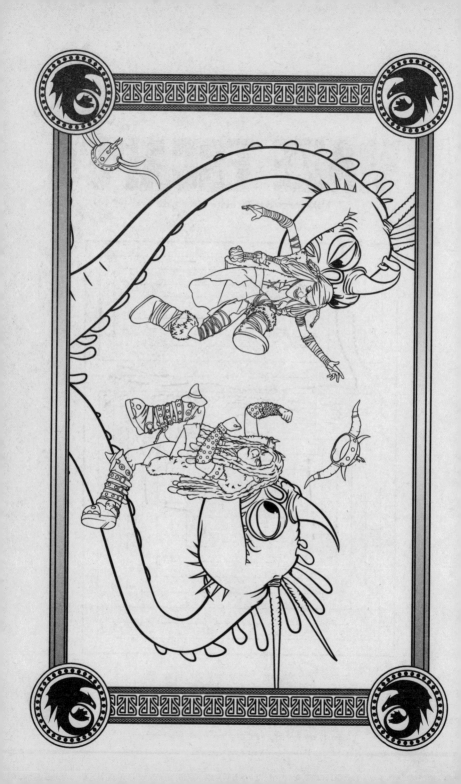

INTERLOCK

Using the words from the list, complete this interlocked word puzzle.

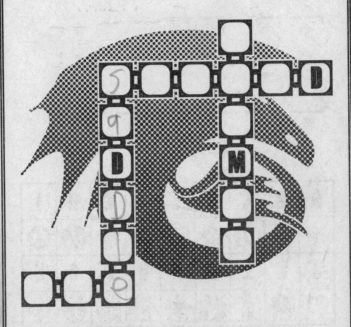

CODEBREAKER

Using the secret code below, fill in the blanks and reveal the hidden words.

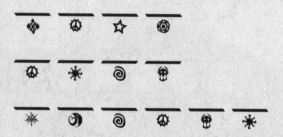

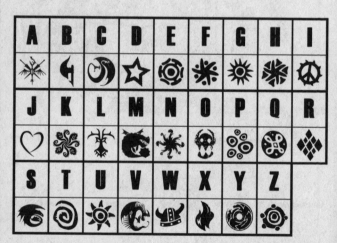

A	B	C	D	E	F	G	H	I
J	K	L	M	N	O	P	Q	R
S	T	U	V	W	X	Y	Z	

PICK A PIECE

Color the piece that completes the puzzle below.

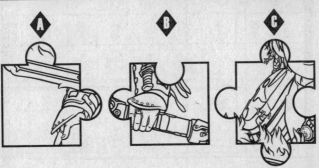

GRID DRAW

Using the grid as a guide,
copy the picture in the grid below.

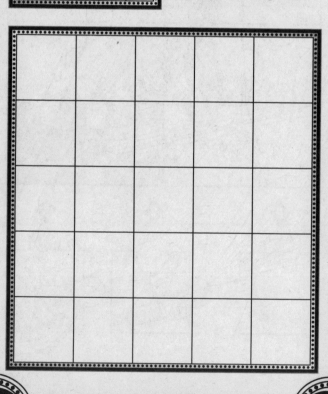

WORD COUNT

How many words can you make using the letters from...

DEFEND THE VILLAGE

Example: left

_____ _____

_____ _____

_____ _____

_____ _____

_____ _____

_____ _____

_____ _____

_____ _____

_____ _____

_____ _____

_____ _____

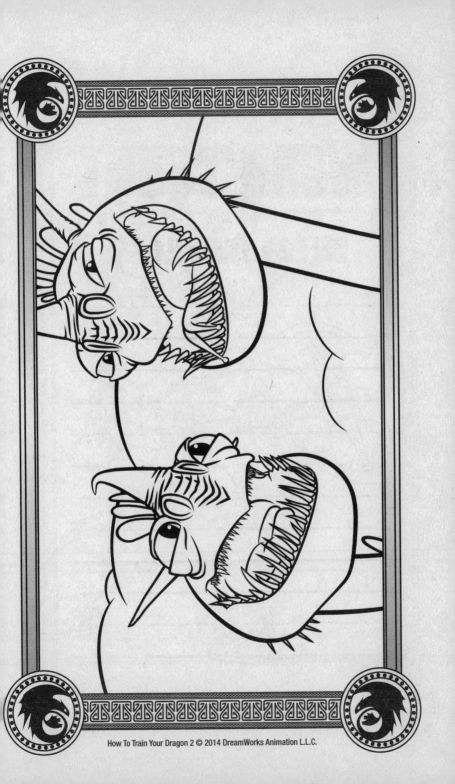

RIDER MATCH

Draw a line between the rider and his or her dragon.

1

2

3

ANSWER: A-3, B-1, C-2

How To Train Your Dragon 2 © 2014 DreamWorks Animation L.L.C.

INTERLOCK

Using the words from the list, complete this interlocked word puzzle.

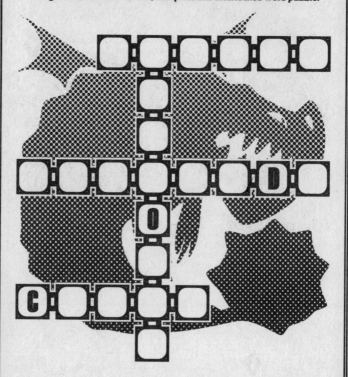

WORD LIST

SECRET   EXPLORER   CAVES   NEW LANDS

MAZE ESCAPE

Help Hiccup through the maze.

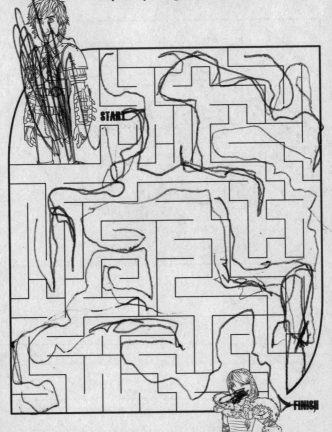

START

FINISH

PICK A PIECE

Color the piece that completes the puzzle below.

A   B   C

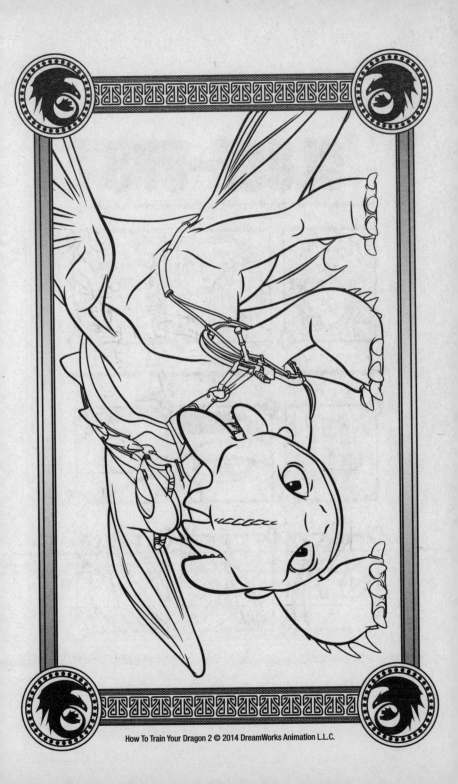

CLOSE-UPS

Match the characters by writing the correct number below each close-up.

CODEBREAKER

Using the secret code below, fill in the blanks and reveal the hidden words.

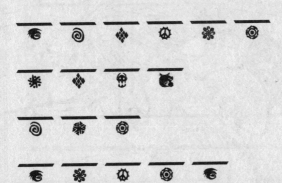

WORD COUNT

How many words can you make using the letters from...

NOT BACKING DOWN

Example: bonk

_____   _____

_____   _____

_____   _____

_____   _____

_____   _____

_____   _____

_____   _____

_____   _____

_____   _____

_____   _____

_____   _____

GRID
DRAW

**Using the grid as a guide,
copy the picture in the grid below.**

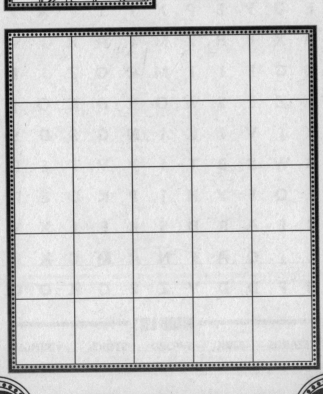

WORD SEARCH

Find the words from the list in the puzzle below.

```
C M T F P K F S H H S
J N Q H R W G R P B W
L U Y E P X I Y F X Y
A X B H Z M T A X I M
Q G F I I M O O Z I E
A Z E S W O R D C Q J
X J V I K I N G S G S
B W B B T I Y V T E D
E Q E Y H J P K O E R
B E A R D S B F I X V
L J Q A F N A M C K B
N P D D V Z E O K O O
```

◄━━━━ **WORD LIST** ━━━━►

BEARDS   **BERK**   **SWORD**   **STOICK**   **VIKINGS**

CODEBREAKER

Using the secret code below, fill in the blanks and reveal the hidden words.

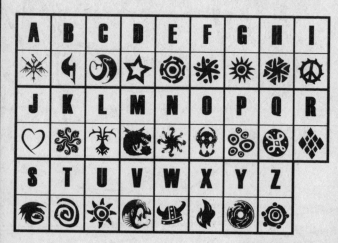

UNSCRAMBLE

Rearrange the scrambled letters to reveal the hidden words.

HFIGLT _____

LDSADE _____

FIRCEE _____

EIDRR _____

RITAN _____

WORD LIST

RIDER   FLIGHT   TRAIN   SADDLE   FIERCE

ANSWERS: Flight, Saddle, Fierce, Rider, Train

CLOSE-UPS

Match the characters by writing the correct number below each close-up.

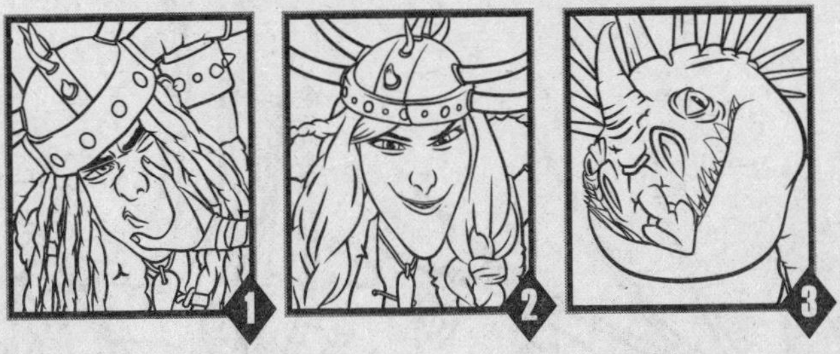

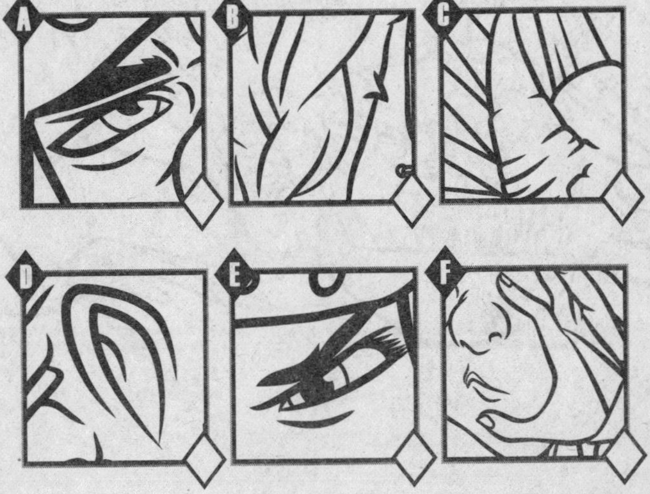

ANSWER: A-1, B-2, C-3, D-3, E-2, F-1

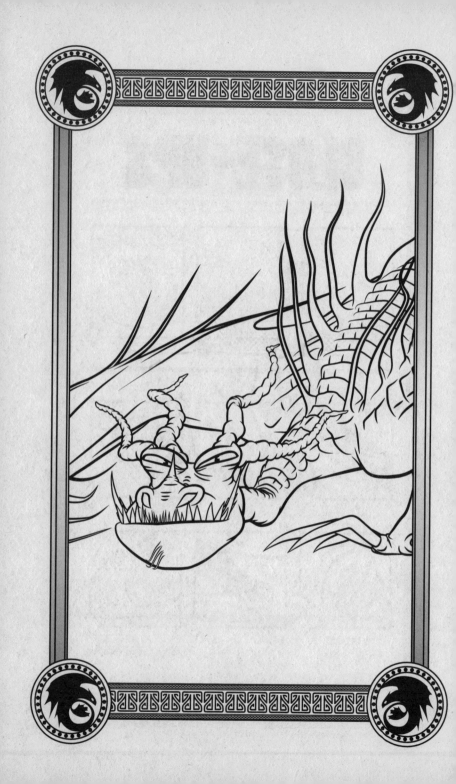

INTERLOCK

Using the words from the list, complete this interlocked word puzzle.

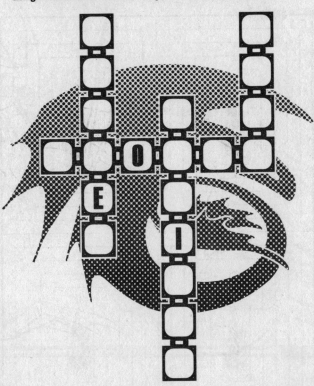

WORD LIST

VIKINGS **BERK** **STOICK** **UNITED**

MAZE ESCAPE

Help Hiccup through the maze while avoiding the fire.

GRID DRAW

Using the grid as a guide,
copy the picture in the grid below.

RIDER MATCH

Draw a line between the rider and his or her dragon.

A

1

B

2

C

3

ANSWER: A-2, B-3, C-1

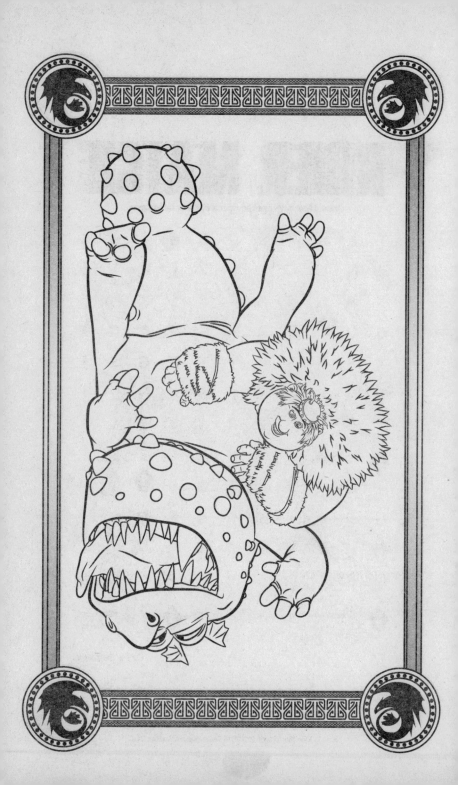

WORD SEARCH

Find the words from the list in the puzzle below.

```
A L H E T G E N J W R
P N C C J L Y J K I J
Y A U A A F X E K N E
D U T G B E W F T G Y
X Y P A L T T V G S J
T U L G U V B K N J I
Y B J C E B S Y E S R
L M W R V E A O E Y T
W U I A K T S L H N A
G F J I M L A F Q I I
N H P S V C O N V H L
T S T Q S B Z A Q D N
```

WORD LIST

FIRE   SCALES   SPIKES   TAIL   WINGS

How To Train Your Dragon 2 © 2014 DreamWorks Animation L.L.C.

INTERLOCK

Using the words from the list, complete this interlocked word puzzle.

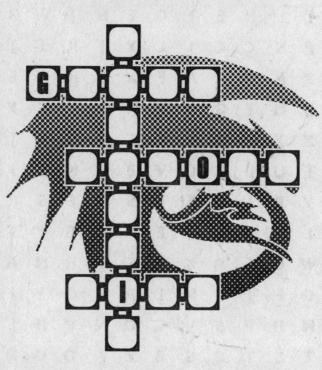

WORD LIST

GRAND   FIRE   HEROIC   MAJESTIC

RIDER MATCH

Draw a line between the rider and his or her dragon.

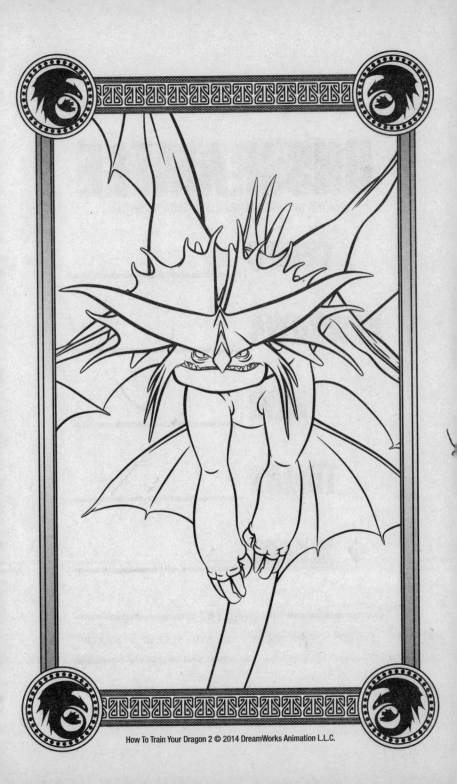

UNSCRAMBLE

Rearrange the scrambled letters to reveal the hidden words.

CUHIPC _____

DAWKRWA _____

DKNI _____

TRMAS _____

IKIVNG _____

WORD LIST

SMART   AWKWARD   VIKING   KIND   HICCUP

MAZE ESCAPE

Help Zippleback through the maze and back to Ruffnut and Tuffnut.

FINISH

START

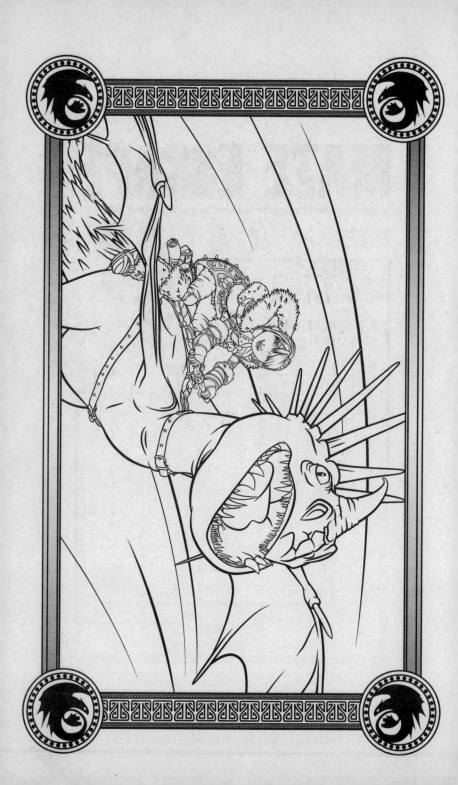

GRID
DRAW

**Using the grid as a guide,
copy the picture in the grid below.**

WORD COUNT

How many words can you make using the letters from...

FOLLOW MY LEAD, BUD!

Example: flood

_____   _____

_____   _____

_____   _____

_____   _____

_____   _____

_____   _____

_____   _____

_____   _____

_____   _____

_____   _____

_____   _____

_____   _____

INTERLOCK

Using the words from the list, complete this interlocked word puzzle.

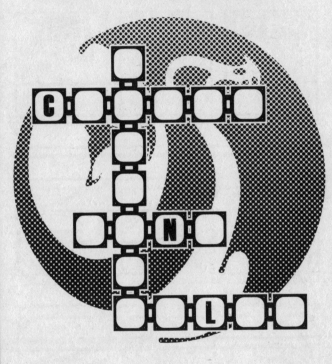

WORD LIST

WIND   SOARING   GALES   CLOUDS

CLOSE-UPS

Match the characters by writing the correct number below each close-up.

1

2

3

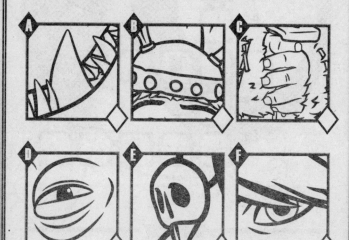

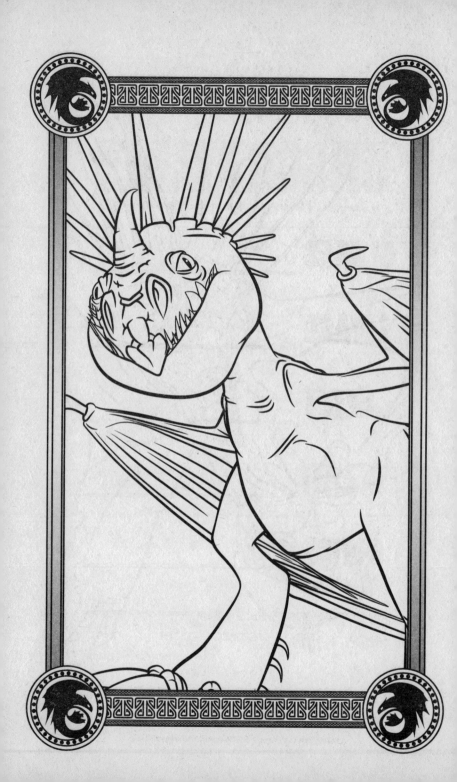

UNSCRAMBLE

Rearrange the scrambled letters to reveal the hidden words.

SLCAES _____

LWASC _____

HETET _____

LATI _____

NWIGS _____

WORD LIST

CLAWS   TAIL   SCALES   TEETH   WINGS

RIDER MATCH

Draw a line between the rider and his or her dragon.

A

1

B

2

C

3

PICK A PIECE

Color the piece that completes the puzzle below.

A   **B**   **C**

RIDER MATCH

Draw a line between the rider and his or her dragon.

TIC-TAC-TOE

Use these grids to challenge your friends.

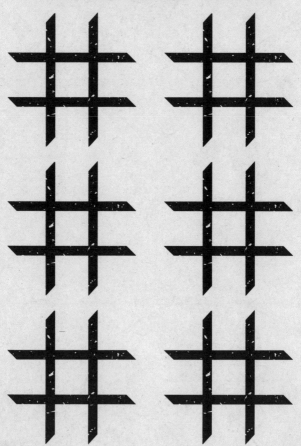

CODEBREAKER

Using the secret code below, fill in the blanks and reveal the hidden words.

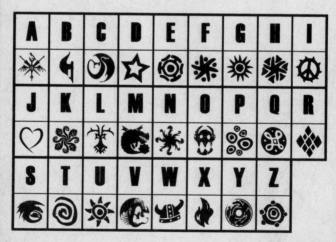

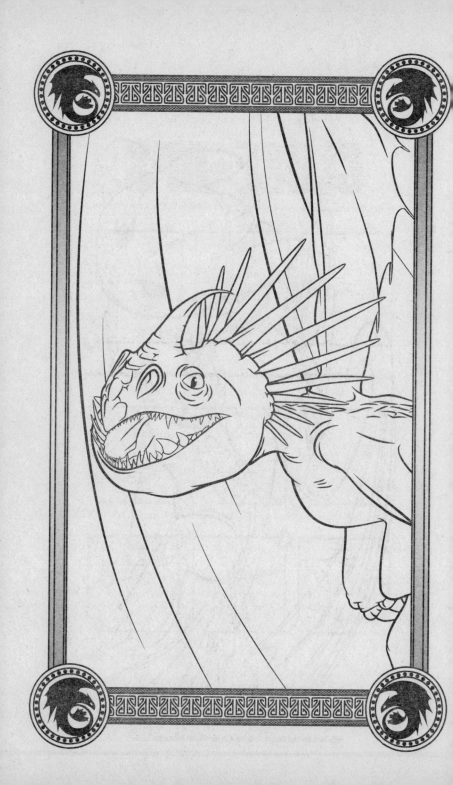

CLOSE-UPS

Match the characters by writing the correct number below each close-up.

1

2

3

 A

 B

 C

 D

 E

 F

ANSWER: A-1, B-2, C-2, D-3, E-3, F-1

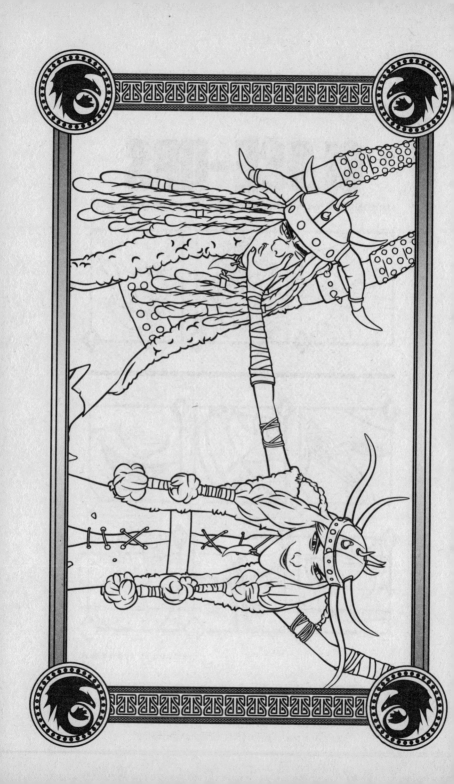

INTERLOCK

Using the words from the list, complete this interlocked word puzzle.

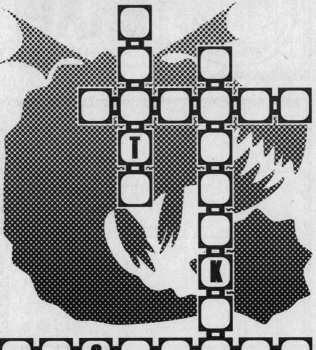

WORD LIST

SCARED   FISHLEGS   GRONCKLE   FACTS

GRID DRAW

Using the grid as a guide,
copy the picture in the grid below.

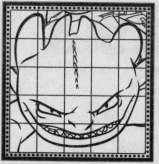

UNSCRAMBLE

Rearrange the scrambled letters to reveal the hidden words.

ERAC _____

PCMOETE _____

NWIRNE _____

FNIIHS _____

AFTS _____

━━━━━◄══ **WORD LIST** ══►━━━━━

FINISH   FAST   COMPETE   RACE   WINNER

PICK A PIECE

Color the piece that completes the puzzle below.

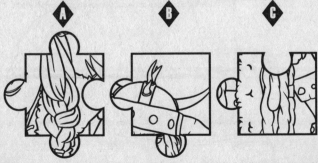

ANSWER: Piece B

WORD SEARCH

Find the words from the list in the puzzle below.

```
E  O  Z  B  E  K  P  U  B  D  U
T  M  H  F  A  V  L  K  J  F  L
N  S  E  P  B  C  T  H  M  D  G
C  L  I  F  F  Y  H  N  O  L  X
J  A  J  G  A  W  T  A  U  H  X
M  B  X  X  A  B  J  M  N  V  Q
J  W  W  G  U  J  D  Y  T  F  V
R  V  F  Q  Y  F  P  S  A  E  D
T  Z  I  G  I  O  A  T  I  U  I
J  Q  G  K  Y  E  K  E  N  I  J
Q  O  P  V  E  O  L  R  S  I  Q
F  I  S  L  A  N  D  Y  A  K  Q
```

⟶ WORD LIST ⟵

CLIFF   FOGGY   ISLAND   MOUNTAINS   MYSTERY

WORD COUNT

How many words can you make using the letters from...

THE BOOK OF DRAGONS

Example: heat

_____   _____

_____   _____

_____   _____

_____   _____

_____   _____

_____   _____

_____   _____

_____   _____

_____   _____

_____   _____

_____   _____

CLOSE-UPS

Match the characters by writing the correct number below each close-up.

1

2

3

INTERLOCK

Using the words from the list, complete this interlocked word puzzle.

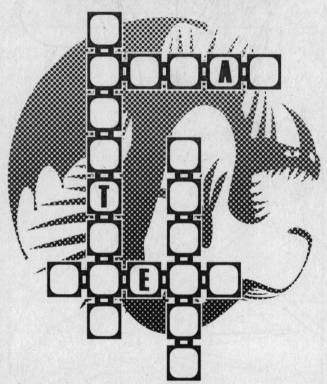

MAZE ESCAPE

Help Astrid through the maze and back to Stormfly.

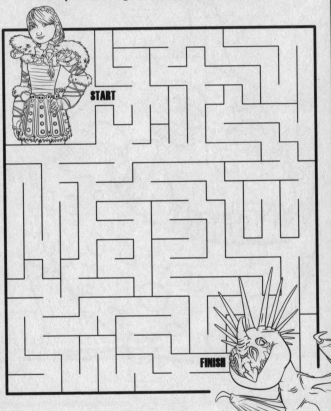

START

FINISH

WORD SEARCH

Find the words from the list in the puzzle below.

```
Q  N  O  R  T  H  W  X  O  L  B
L  I  M  C  A  J  Q  K  P  C  N
A  B  Q  Q  P  P  M  N  Y  D  U
I  O  Z  R  O  U  T  E  N  M  D
K  Z  X  O  A  Y  G  E  T  A  G
E  M  R  B  T  A  G  L  A  R  F
I  E  A  W  I  E  P  B  T  U  F
N  Z  N  P  L  N  G  N  T  D  O
V  K  O  G  T  F  Z  B  E  K  V
N  E  Z  F  W  F  G  Q  R  N  A
S  A  T  M  L  R  B  R  E  X  K
F  N  K  Z  T  R  C  T  D  W  O
```

◆━━ WORD LIST ━━◆

LEGEND   MAP   NORTH   ROUTE   TATTERED

How To Train Your Dragon 2 © 2014 DreamWorks Animation L.L.C.

UNSCRAMBLE

Rearrange the scrambled letters to reveal the hidden words.

SIANLD _____

EBRK _____

PLOERXE _____

FCIHE _____

EAVC _____

◆━━━━ **WORD LIST** ━━━━◆

CHIEF   EXPLORE   CAVE   ISLAND   BERK

RIDER MATCH

Draw a line between the rider and his or her dragon.

MAZE ESCAPE

Help Astrid and Stormfly through the maze and back to Hiccup and Toothless.

START

FINISH

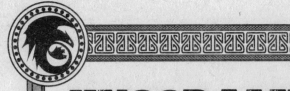

UNSCRAMBLE

Rearrange the scrambled letters to reveal the hidden words.

MHUNAS _____

SRADNGO _____

NUITE _____

TTEOHGRE _____

CPAEE _____

═══════◆═══════ **WORD LIST** ═══════◆═══════

UNITE   DRAGONS   PEACE   TOGETHER   HUMANS

INTERLOCK

Using the words from the list, complete this interlocked word puzzle.

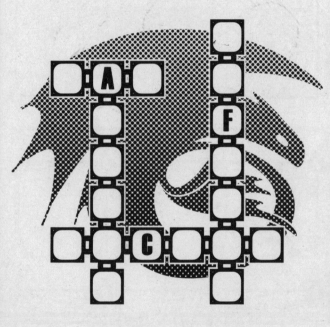

WORD LIST

HICCUP   TUFFNUT   ASTRID   PAL

CLOSE-UPS

Match the characters by writing the correct number below each close-up.

RIDER MATCH

Draw a line between the rider and his or her dragon.

A

1

B

2

C

3

ANSWER: A-2, B-3, C-1

WORD COUNT

How many words can you make using the letters from...

CERTIFIED DRAGON TRAINER

Example: drift

_____   _____

_____   _____

_____   _____

_____   _____

_____   _____

_____   _____

_____   _____

_____   _____

_____   _____

_____   _____

_____   _____

_____   _____

CODEBREAKER

Using the secret code below, fill in the blanks and reveal the hidden words.

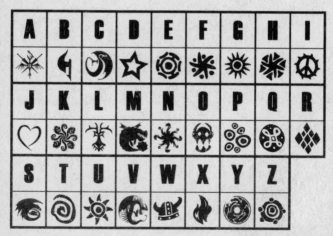

GRID DRAW

Using the grid as a guide,
copy the picture in the grid below.

PICK A PIECE

Color the piece that completes the puzzle below.

CODEBREAKER

Using the secret code below, fill in the blanks and reveal the hidden words.

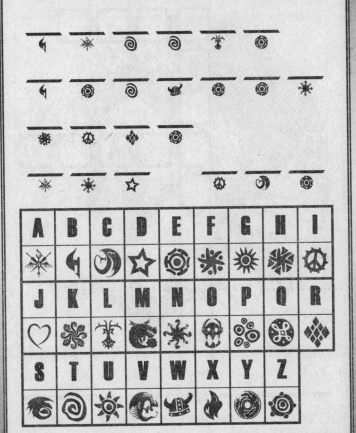

INTERLOCK

Using the words from the list, complete this interlocked word puzzle.

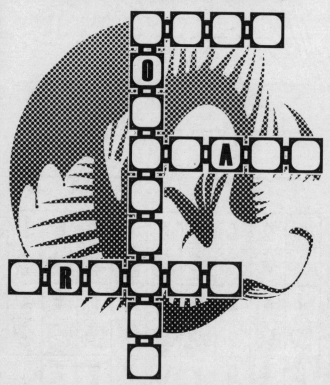

WORD LIST

TRAIN   TOOTHLESS   FRIEND   TAIL

MAZE ESCAPE

Help Hiccup and Toothless through the maze and back to Snotlout and Hookfang.

START

FINISH

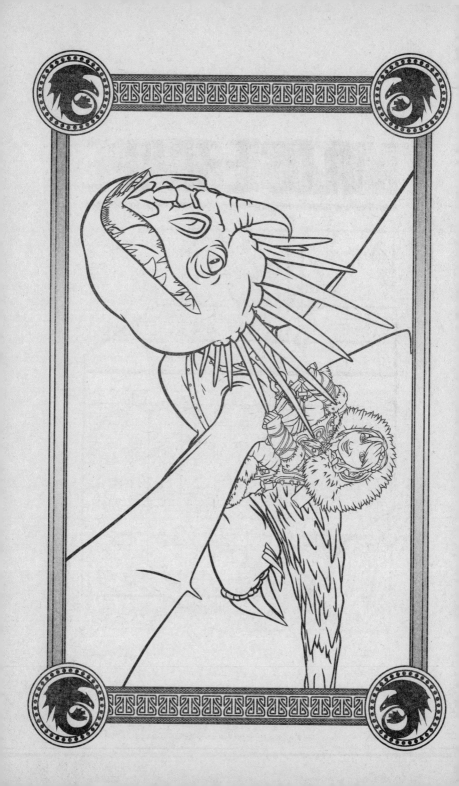

CLOSE-UPS

Match the characters by writing the correct number below each close-up.

1

2

3

A

B

C

D

E

F

GRID DRAW

Using the grid as a guide,
copy the picture in the grid below.

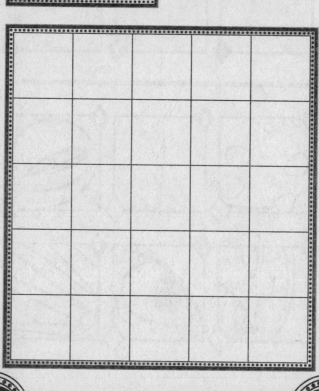

RIDER MATCH

Draw a line between the rider and his or her dragon.

A

1

B

2

C

3

ANSWER: A-3, B-1, C-2

How To Train Your Dragon 2 © 2014 DreamWorks Animation L.L.C.

INTERLOCK

Using the words from the list, complete this interlocked word puzzle.

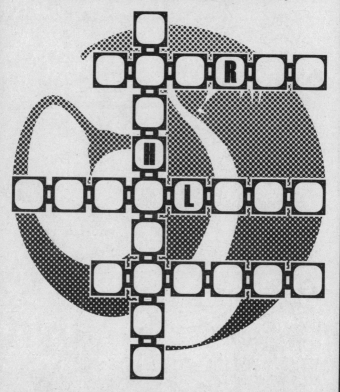

WORD LIST

HAMMER   **SNOTLOUT**   **FIERCE**   **NIGHTMARE**

WORD COUNT

How many words can you make using the letters from...

AWESOME IN ACTION

Example: cans

_____   _____

_____   _____

_____   _____

_____   _____

_____   _____

_____   _____

_____   _____

_____   _____

_____   _____

_____   _____

_____   _____

PICK A PIECE

Color the piece that completes the puzzle below.

◆ **A** ◆   ◆ **B** ◆   ◆ **C** ◆

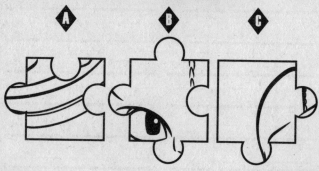

CODEBREAKER

Using the secret code below, fill in the blanks and reveal the hidden words.

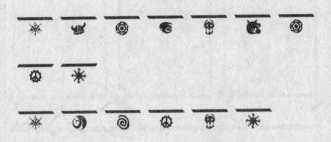

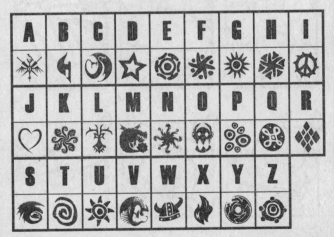

CLOSE-UPS

Match the characters by writing the correct number below each close-up.

 **1**

 **2**

 **3**

 **A**

 **B**

 **C**

 **D**

 **E**

 **F**

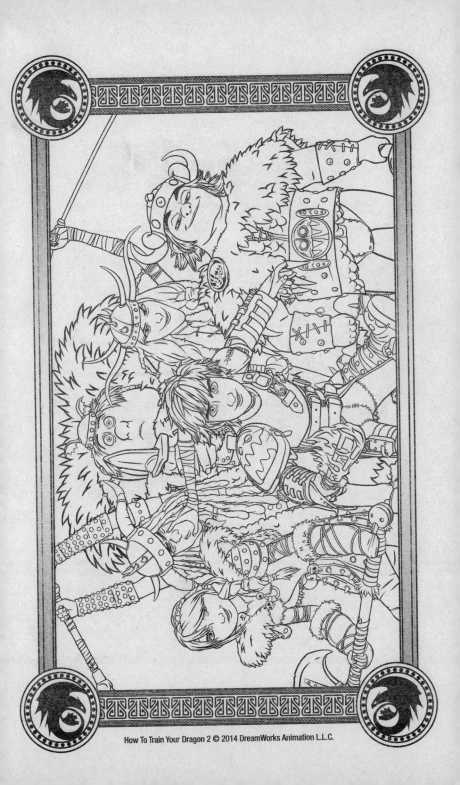

How To Train Your Dragon 2 © 2014 DreamWorks Animation L.L.C.